MEDITERRANEAN DIET SEAFOOD RECIPES

LEARN HOW TO COOK MEDITERRANEAN THROUGH THIS DETAILED COOKBOOK, COMPLETE OF SEVERAL TASTY IDEAS FOR GOOD AND HEALTY SEAFOOD RECIPES. SUITABLE FOT BOYTH ADULTS AND KIDS, IT WILL HELP YOU LOSE WEIGHT AND FEEL BETTER, WITHOUT GIVING UP YOUR FAVOURITE FOOD

Table of Contents

Salmon and Lemon Peaches Bowls

Prep time: 10 minutes I **Cooking time:** 0 minutes I **Servings:** 4

Ingredients:
- 2 salmon fillets, boneless, skinless and cubed
- 2 peaches, stones removed and cubed
- 1 teaspoon olive oil
- A pinch of black pepper
- 2 cups baby spinach
- ½ tablespoon balsamic vinegar
- 1 tablespoon lemon juice
- 1 tablespoon cilantro, chopped

Directions:
1. In a salad bowl, combine the salmon with the peaches and the other ingredients, toss and serve cold.

Nutrition info per serving: calories 133, fat 7.1, fiber 1.5, carbs 8.2, protein 1.7

Coconut Salmon

Prep time: 10 minutes I **Cooking time:** 15 minutes I **Servings:** 4

Ingredients:
- 2 tablespoons olive oil
- 4 salmon fillets, boneless
- 1 tablespoon capers, drained
- 1 tablespoon dill, chopped
- 1 shallot, chopped
- ½ cup coconut cream
- A pinch of black pepper

Directions:
1. Heat up a pan with the oil over medium-high heat, add the shallot and the capers, toss and sauté fro 4 minutes.
2. Add the salmon and cook it for 3 minutes on each side.
3. Add the rest of the ingredients, cook everything for 5 minutes more, divide between plates and serve.

Nutrition info per serving: calories 369, fat 25.2, fiber 0.9, carbs 2.7, protein 35.5

Salmon Salad

Prep time: 10 minutes I **Cooking time:** 0 minutes I **Servings:** 4

Ingredients:
- 2 tablespoons olive oil
- ½ teaspoon lemon juice
- ½ teaspoon lemon zest, grated
- A pinch of black pepper
- 1 cup black olives, pitted and halved
- 1 cup cucumber, cubed
- ½ pound salmon, boiled, boneless and cubed
- 1 tablespoon chives, chopped

Directions:
1. In a salad bowl, combine the salmon with the olives and the other ingredients, toss and serve.

Nutrition info per serving: calories 170, fat 13.1, fiber 1.3, carbs 3.2, protein 10.9

Lime Tuna Mix

Prep time: 10 minutes I **Cooking time:** 15 minutes I **Servings:** 4

Ingredients:
- 4 tuna fillets, boneless and skinless
- 1 tablespoon olive oil
- 2 shallots, chopped
- 2 tablespoons lime juice
- A pinch of black pepper
- 1 teaspoon sweet paprika
- ½ cup chicken stock

Directions:
1. Heat up a pan with the oil over medium-high heat, add shallots and sauté for 3 minutes.
2. Add the fish and cook it for 4 minutes on each side.
3. Add the rest of the ingredients, cook everything for 3 minutes more, divide between plates and serve.

Nutrition info per serving: calories 404, fat 34.6, fiber 0.3, carbs 3, protein 21.4

Cod and Shallot Mix

Prep time: 10 minutes I **Cooking time:** 17 minutes I **Servings:** 4

Ingredients:
- 2 tablespoons olive oil
- 1 tablespoon lemon juice
- 1 tablespoon mint, chopped
- 4 cod fillets, boneless
- 1 teaspoons lemon zest, grated
- A pinch of black pepper
- ¼ cup shallot, chopped
- ½ cup chicken stock

Directions:
1. Heat up a pan with the oil over medium heat, add the shallots, stir and sauté for 5 minutes.
2. Add the cod, the lemon juice and the other ingredients, bring to a simmer and cook over medium heat for 12 minutes.
3. Divide everything between plates and serve.

Nutrition info per serving: calories 160, fat 8.1, fiber 0.2, carbs 2, protein 20.5

Garlic Cod and Tomatoes

Prep time: 10 minutes I **Cooking time:** 16 minutes I **Servings:** 4

Ingredients:
- 2 tablespoons olive oil
- 2 garlic cloves, minced
- ½ cup veggie stock
- 4 cod fillets, boneless
- 1 cup cherry tomatoes, halved
- 2 tablespoons lime juice
- A pinch of black pepper
- 1 tablespoon chives, chopped

Directions:
1. Heat up a pan with the oil over medium-high heat, add the garlic and the fish and cook for 3 minutes on each side.
2. Add the rest of the ingredients, bring to a simmer and cook over medium heat for 10 minutes more.
3. Divide everything between plates and serve.

Nutrition info per serving: calories 169, fat 8.1, fiber 0.8, carbs 4.7, protein 20.7

Chili Tuna

Prep time: 4 minutes I **Cooking time:** 10 minutes I **Servings:** 4

Ingredients:
- 2 tablespoons olive oil
- 4 tuna steaks, boneless
- 2 teaspoons sweet paprika
- ½ teaspoon chili powder
- A pinch of black pepper

Directions:
1. Heat up a pan with the oil over medium-high heat, add the tuna steaks, season with paprika, black pepper and chili powder, cook for 5 minutes on each side, divide between plates and serve with a side salad.

Nutrition info per serving: calories 455, fat 20.6, fiber 0.5, carbs 0.8, protein 63.8

Balsamic Cod and Spring Onions

Prep time: 5 minutes I **Cooking time:** 12 minutes I **Servings:** 4

Ingredients:
- 1 tablespoon parsley, chopped
- 4 cod fillets, boneless
- 1 cup orange juice
- 2 spring onions, chopped
- 1 teaspoon orange zest, grated
- 1 tablespoon olive oil
- 1 teaspoon balsamic vinegar
- A pinch of black pepper

Directions:
1. Heat up a pan with the oil over medium heat, add the spring onions, and sauté for 2 minutes.
2. Add the fish and the other ingredients, cook for 5 minutes on each side, divide everything between plates and serve.

Nutrition info per serving: calories 152, fat 4.7, fiber 0.4, carbs 7.2, protein 20.6

Basil Garlic Salmon

Prep time: 5 minutes I **Cooking time:** 14 minutes I **Servings:** 4

Ingredients:
- 2 tablespoons olive oil
- 4 salmon fillets, skinless
- 2 garlic cloves, minced
- A pinch of black pepper
- 2 tablespoons balsamic vinegar
- 2 tablespoons basil, chopped

Directions:
1. Heat up a pan with the olive oil, add the fish and cook for 4 minutes on each side.
2. Add the rest of the ingredients, cook everything for 6 minutes more.
3. Divide everything between plates and serve.

Nutrition info per serving: calories 300, fat 18, fiber 0.1, carbs 0.6, protein 34.7

Yogurt Cod Mix

Prep time: 10 minutes I **Cooking time:** 15 minutes I **Servings:** 4

Ingredients:
- 2 tablespoons olive oil
- 4 cod fillets, boneless and skinless
- 1 shallot, chopped
- ½ cup coconut cream
- 3 tablespoons Greek yogurt
- 2 tablespoons dill, chopped
- A pinch of black pepper
- 1 garlic clove minced

Directions:
1. Heat up a pan with the oil over medium heat, add the shallots and sauté for 5 minutes.
2. Add the fish and the other ingredients, and cook for 10 minutes more.
3. Divide everything between plates and serve.

Nutrition info per serving: calories 252, fat 15.2, fiber 0.9, carbs 7.7, protein 22.3

Halibut and Tomatoes Mix

Prep time: 10 minutes I **Cooking time:** 15 minutes I **Servings:** 4

Ingredients:
- 2 shallots, chopped
- 4 halibut fillets, boneless
- 1 cup radishes, halved
- 1 cup tomatoes, cubed
- 1 tablespoon olive oil
- 1 tablespoon cilantro, chopped
- 2 teaspoons lemon juice
- A pinch of black pepper

Directions:
1. Grease a roasting pan with the oil and arrange the fish inside.
2. Add the rest of the ingredients, introduce in the oven and bake at 400 degrees F for 15 minutes.
3. Divide everything between plates and serve.

Nutrition info per serving: calories 231, fat 7.8, fiber 6, carbs 11.9, protein 21.1

Parsley Salmon Mix

Prep time: 10 minutes I **Cooking time:** 15 minutes I **Servings:** 4

Ingredients:
- 2 tablespoons olive oil
- ½ cup almonds, chopped
- 4 salmon fillets, boneless
- 1 shallot, chopped
- ½ cup veggie stock
- 2 tablespoons parsley, chopped
- Black pepper to the taste

=
Directions:
1. Heat up a pan with the oil over medium heat, add the shallot and sauté for 4 minutes.
2. Add the salmon and the other ingredients, cook for 5 minutes on each side, divide everything between plates and serve.

Nutrition info per serving: calories 240, fat 6.4, fiber 2.6, carbs 11.4, protein 15

Cod and Veggies

Prep time: 10 minutes I **Cooking time:** 20 minutes I **Servings:** 4

Ingredients:
- 2 tablespoons coconut aminos
- 1 pound broccoli florets
- 4 cod fillets, boneless
- 1 red onion, chopped
- 2 tablespoons olive oil
- ¼ cup chicken stock
- Black pepper to the taste

Directions:
1. Heat up a pan with the oil over medium heat, add the onion and the broccoli and cook for 5 minutes.
2. Add the fish and the other ingredients, cook for 20 minutes more, divide everything between plates and serve.

Nutrition info per serving: calories 220, fat 14.3, fiber 6.3, carbs 16.2, protein 9

Cilantro Sea Bass

Prep time: 10 minutes I **Cooking time:** 15 minutes I **Servings:** 4

Ingredients:
- 1 tablespoon balsamic vinegar
- 1 tablespoon ginger, grated
- 2 tablespoons olive oil
- Black pepper to the taste
- 4 sea bass fillets, boneless
- 1 tablespoon cilantro, chopped

Directions:
1. Heat up a pan with the oil over medium heat, add the fish and cook for 5 minutes on each side.
2. Add the rest of the ingredients, cook everything for 5 minutes more, divide everything between plates and serve.

Nutrition info per serving: calories 267, fat 11.2, fiber 5.2, carbs 14.3, protein 14.3

Balsamic Salmon and Beans

Prep time: 10 minutes I **Cooking time:** 20 minutes I **Servings:** 4

Ingredients:
- 2 tablespoons olive oil
- 1 cup chicken stock
- 4 salmon fillets, boneless
- 2 garlic cloves, minced
- 1 tablespoon ginger, grated
- ½ pound green beans, trimmed and halved
- 2 teaspoons balsamic vinegar
- ¼ cup scallions, chopped

Directions:
1. Heat up a pan with the oil over medium heat, add the scallion and the garlic and sauté for 5 minutes.
2. Add the salmon and cook it for 5 minutes on each side.
3. Add the rest of the ingredients, cook everything for 5 minutes more, divide between plates and serve.

Nutrition info per serving: calories 220, fat 11.6, fiber 2, carbs 17.2, protein 9.3

Parsley Shrimp Mix

Prep time: 10 minutes I **Cooking time:** 10 minutes I **Servings:** 4

Ingredients:
- 1 tablespoon olive oil
- 1 pound shrimp, peeled and deveined
- 1 cup pineapple, peeled and cubed
- Juice of 1 lemon
- A bunch of parsley, chopped

Directions:
1. Heat up a pan with the oil over medium heat, add the shrimp and cook for 3 minutes on each side.
2. Add the rest of the ingredients, cook everything for 4 minutes more, divide into bowls and serve.

Nutrition info per serving: calories 254, fat 13.3, fiber 6, carbs 14.9, protein 11

Chives Salmon and Olives

Prep time: 10 minutes I **Cooking time:** 20 minutes I **Servings:** 4

Ingredients:
- 1 yellow onion, chopped
- 1 cup green olives, pitted and halved
- 1 teaspoon chili powder
- Black pepper to the taste
- 2 tablespoons olive oil
- ¼ cup veggie stock
- 4 salmon fillets, skinless and boneless
- 2 tablespoons chives, chopped

Directions:
1. Heat up a pan with the oil over medium-high heat, add the onion and sauté for 3 minutes.
2. Add the salmon and cook for 5 minutes on each side.
   Add the rest of the ingredients, cook the mix for 5 minutes more, divide between plates and serve.

Nutrition info per serving: calories 221, fat 12.1, fiber 5.4, carbs 8.5, protein 11.2

Lemon Salmon and Endives

Prep time: 5 minutes I **Cooking time:** 15 minutes I **Servings:** 4

Ingredients:
- 4 medium salmon fillets, skinless and boneless
- 2 endives, shredded
- ½ cup veggie stock
- 2 tablespoons olive oil
- Black pepper to the taste
- 1 tablespoon lemon juice
- 1 tablespoon cilantro, chopped

Directions:
1. Heat up a pan with the oil over medium heat, add the endives and cook for 3 minutes.
2. Add the fish and brown it for 4 minutes on each side.
3. Add the rest of the ingredients, cook everything for 4 minutes more, divide between plates and serve.

Nutrition info per serving: calories 252, fat 9.3, fiber 4.2, carbs 12.3, protein 9

Coconut Cod and Asparagus

Prep time: 10 minutes I **Cooking time:** 14 minutes I **Servings:** 4

Ingredients:
- 1 tablespoon olive oil
- 1 red onion, chopped
- 1 pound cod fillets, boneless
- 1 bunch asparagus, trimmed
- Black pepper to the taste
- 1 cup coconut cream
- 1 tablespoon chives, chopped

Directions:
1. Heat up a pan with the oil over medium heat, add the onion and the cod and cook it for 3 minutes on each side.
2. Add the rest of the ingredients, cook everything for 8 minutes more, divide between plates and serve.

Nutrition info per serving: calories 254, fat 12.1, fiber 5.4, carbs 4.2, protein 13.5

Cumin Shrimp

Prep time: 5 minutes I **Cooking time:** 8 minutes I **Servings:** 4

Ingredients:
- 1 teaspoon garlic powder
- 1 teaspoon smoked paprika
- 1 teaspoon cumin, ground
- 1 teaspoon allspice, ground
- 2 tablespoons olive oil
- 2 pounds shrimp, peeled and deveined
- 1 tablespoon chives, chopped

Directions:
1. Heat up a pan with the oil over medium heat, add the shrimp, garlic powder and the other ingredients, cook for 4 minutes on each side, divide into bowls and serve.

Nutrition info per serving: calories 212, fat 9.6, fiber 5.3, carbs 12.7, protein 15.4

Sea Bass Mix

Prep time: 10 minutes I **Cooking time:** 30 minutes I **Servings:** 4

Ingredients:
- 2 tablespoons olive oil
- 2 pounds sea bass fillets, skinless and boneless
- Black pepper to the taste
- 2 cups cherry tomatoes, halved
- 1 tablespoon chives, chopped
- 1 tablespoon lemon zest, grated
- ¼ cup lemon juice

Directions:
1. Grease a roasting pan with the oil and arrange the fish inside.
2. Add the tomatoes and the other ingredients, introduce the pan in the oven and bake at 380 degrees F for 30 minutes.
3. Divide everything between plates and serve.

Nutrition info per serving: calories 272, fat 6.9, fiber 6.2, carbs 18.4, protein 9

Oregano Shrimp

Prep time: 10 minutes I **Cooking time:** 12 minutes I **Servings:** 4

Ingredients:
- 1 pound shrimp, deveined and peeled
- 1 tablespoon olive oil
- Juice of 1 lime
- 1 cup black beans, cooked
- 1 shallot, chopped
- 1 tablespoon oregano, chopped
- 2 garlic cloves, chopped
- Black pepper to the taste

Directions:
1. Heat up a pan with the oil over medium-high heat, add the shallot and the garlic, stir and cook for 3 minutes.
2. Add the shrimp and cook for 2 minutes on each side.
3. Add the beans and the other ingredients, cook everything over medium heat for 5 minutes more, divide into bowls and serve.

Nutrition info per serving: calories 253, fat 11.6, fiber 6, carbs 14.5, protein 13.5

Shrimp and Shallots

Prep time: 5 minutes I **Cooking time:** 8 minutes I **Servings:** 4

Ingredients:
- 1 pound shrimp, peeled and deveined
- 2 shallots, chopped
- 1 tablespoon olive oil
- 1 tablespoon chives, chopped
- 2 teaspoons prepared horseradish
- ¼ cup coconut cream
- Black pepper to the taste

Directions:
1. Heat up a pan with the oil over medium heat, add the shallots and the horseradish, stir and sauté for 2 minutes.
2. Add the shrimp and the other ingredients, toss, cook for 6 minutes more, divide between plates and serve.

Nutrition info per serving: calories 233, fat 6, fiber 5, carbs 11.9, protein 5.4

Shrimp and Capers Salad

Prep time: 4 minutes I **Cooking time:** 0 minutes I **Servings:** 4

Ingredients:
- 1 pound shrimp, cooked, peeled and deveined
- 1 tablespoon tarragon, chopped
- 1 tablespoon capers, drained
- 2 tablespoons olive oil
- Black pepper to the taste
- 2 cups baby spinach
- 1 tablespoon balsamic vinegar
- 1 small red onion, sliced
- 2 tablespoons lemon juice

Directions:
1. In a bowl, combine the shrimp with the tarragon and the other ingredients, toss and serve.

Nutrition info per serving: calories 258, fat 12.4, fiber 6, carbs 6.7, protein 13.3

Cheesy Cod Mix

Prep time: 10 minutes I **Cooking time:** 20 minutes I **Servings:** 4

Ingredients:
- 4 cod fillets, boneless
- ½ cup parmesan cheese, shredded
- 3 garlic cloves, minced
- 1 tablespoon olive oil
- 1 tablespoon lemon juice
- ½ cup green onion, chopped

Directions:
1. Heat up a pan with the oil over medium heat, add the garlic and the green onions, toss and sauté for 5 minutes.
2. Add the fish and cook it for 4 minutes on each side.
3. Add the lemon juice, sprinkle the parmesan on top, cook everything for 2 minutes more, divide between plates and serve.

Nutrition info per serving: calories 275, fat 22.1, fiber 5, carbs 18.2, protein 12

Lemony Tilapia Mix

Prep time: 10 minutes I **Cooking time:** 15 minutes I **Servings:** 4

Ingredients:
- 4 tilapia fillets, boneless
- 2 tablespoons olive oil
- 1 tablespoon lemon juice
- 2 teaspoons lemon zest, grated
- 2 red onions, roughly chopped
- 3 tablespoons chives, chopped

Directions:
1. Heat up a pan with the oil over medium heat, add the onions, lemon zest and lemon juice, toss and sauté for 5 minutes.
2. Add the fish and the chives, cook for 5 minutes on each side, divide between plates and serve.

Nutrition info per serving: calories 254, fat 18.2, fiber 5.4, carbs 11.7, protein 4.5

Trout and Avocado Salad

Prep time: 6 minutes I **Cooking time:** 0 minutes I **Servings:** 4

Ingredients:
- 4 ounces smoked trout, skinless, boneless and cubed
- 1 tablespoon lime juice
- 1/3 cup yogurt
- 2 avocados, peeled, pitted and cubed
- 3 tablespoons chives, chopped
- Black pepper to the taste
- 1 tablespoon olive oil

Directions:
1. In a bowl, combine the trout with the avocados and the other ingredients, toss, and serve.

Nutrition info per serving: calories 244, fat 9.45, fiber 5.6, carbs 8.5, protein 15

Garlic Trout

Prep time: 5 minutes I **Cooking time:** 15 minutes I **Servings:** 4

Ingredients:
- 3 tablespoons balsamic vinegar
- 2 tablespoons olive oil
- 4 trout fillets, boneless
- 3 tablespoons parsley, finely chopped
- 2 garlic cloves, minced

Directions:
1. Heat up a pan with the oil over medium heat, add the trout and cook for 6 minutes on each side.
2. Add the rest of the ingredients, cook for 3 minutes more, divide between plates and serve with a side salad.

Nutrition info per serving: calories 314, fat 14.3, fiber 8.2, carbs 14.8, protein 11.2

Parsley Salmon

Prep time: 5 minutes I **Cooking time:** 12 minutes I **Servings:** 4

Ingredients:
- 2 spring onions, chopped
- 2 teaspoons lime juice
- 1 tablespoon chives, minced
- 1 tablespoon olive oil
- 4 salmon fillets, boneless
- Black pepper to the taste
- 2 tablespoons parsley, chopped

Directions:
1. Heat up a pan with the oil over medium heat, add the spring onions, stir and sauté for 2 minutes.
2. Add the salmon and the other ingredients, cook for 5 minutes on each side, divide between plates and serve.

Nutrition info per serving: calories 290, fat 14.4, fiber 5.6, carbs 15.6, protein 9.5

Trout and Arugula Salad

Prep time: 5 minutes I **Cooking time:** 0 minutes I **Servings:** 4

Ingredients:
- 2 tablespoons olive oil
- ½ cup kalamata olives, pitted and minced
- Black pepper to the taste
- 1 pound smoked trout, boneless, skinless and cubed
- ½ teaspoon lemon zest, grated
- 1 tablespoon lemon juice
- 1 cup cherry tomatoes, halved
- ½ red onion, sliced
- 2 cups baby arugula

Directions:
1. In a bowl, combine smoked trout with the olives, black pepper and the other ingredients, toss and serve.

Nutrition info per serving: calories 282, fat 13.4, fiber 5.3, carbs 11.6, protein 5.6

Saffron Paprika Salmon

Prep time: 10 minutes I **Cooking time:** 12 minutes I **Servings:** 4

Ingredients:
- Black pepper to the taste
- ½ teaspoon sweet paprika
- 4 salmon fillets, boneless
- 3 tablespoons olive oil
- 1 yellow onion, chopped
- 2 garlic cloves, minced
- ¼ teaspoon saffron powder

Directions:
1. Heat up a pan with the oil over medium-high heat, add the onion and the garlic, toss and sauté for 2 minutes.
2. Add the salmon and the other ingredients, cook for 5 minutes on each side, divide between plates and serve.

Nutrition info per serving: calories 339, fat 21.6, fiber 0.7, carbs 3.2, protein 35

Shrimp and Basil Salad

Prep time: 10 minutes I **Cooking time:** 0 minutes I **Servings:** 4

Ingredients:
- ¼ cup basil, chopped
- 2 cups watermelon, peeled and cubed
- 2 tablespoons balsamic vinegar
- 2 tablespoons olive oil
- 1 pound shrimp, peeled, deveined and cooked
- Black pepper to the taste
- 1 tablespoon parsley, chopped

Directions:
1. In a bowl, combine the shrimp with the watermelon and the other ingredients, toss and serve.

Nutrition info per serving: calories 220, fat 9, fiber 0.4, carbs 7.6, protein 26.4

Shrimp and Quinoa Salad

Prep time: 5 minutes I **Cooking time:** 8 minutes I **Servings:** 4

Ingredients:
- 1 pound shrimp, peeled and deveined
- 1 cup quinoa, cooked
- Black pepper to the taste
- 1 tablespoon olive oil
- 1 tablespoon oregano, chopped
- 1 red onion, chopped
- Juice of 1 lemon

Directions:
1. Heat up a pan with the oil over medium-high heat, add the onion, stir and sauté for 2 minutes.
2. Add the shrimp, toss and cook for 5 minutes.
3. Add the rest of the ingredients, toss, divide everything into bowls and serve.

Nutrition info per serving: calories 336, fat 8.2, fiber 4.1, carbs 32.3, protein 32.3

Crab and Cherry Tomato Salad

Prep time: 10 minutes I **Cooking time:** 0 minutes I **Servings:** 4

Ingredients:
- 1 tablespoon olive oil
- 2 cups crab meat
- Black pepper to the taste
- 1 cup cherry tomatoes, halved
- 1 shallot, chopped
- 1 tablespoon lemon juice
- 1/3 cup cilantro, chopped

Directions:
1. In a bowl, combine the crab with the tomatoes and the other ingredients, toss and serve.

Nutrition info per serving: calories 54, fat 3.9, fiber 0.6, carbs 2.6, protein 2.3

Scallops and Scallions

Prep time: 4 minutes I **Cooking time:** 6 minutes I **Servings:** 4

Ingredients:
- 12 ounces sea scallops
- 2 tablespoons olive oil
- 2 garlic cloves, minced
- 1 tablespoon balsamic vinegar
- 1 cup scallions, sliced
- 2 tablespoons cilantro, chopped

Directions:
1. Heat up a pan with the oil over medium heat, add the scallions and the garlic and sauté for 2 minutes.
2. Add the scallops and the other ingredients, cook them for 2 minutes on each side, divide between plates and serve.

Nutrition info per serving: calories 146, fat 7.7, fiber 0.7, carbs 4.4, protein 14.8

Dill Flounder Mix

Prep time: 10 minutes I **Cooking time:** 20 minutes I **Servings:** 4

Ingredients:
- 2 tablespoon olive oil
- 1 red onion, chopped
- Black pepper to the taste
- ½ cup veggie stock
- 4 flounder fillets, boneless
- ½ cup coconut cream
- 1 tablespoon dill, chopped

Directions:
1. Heat up a pan with the oil over medium heat, add the onion, stir and sauté for 5 minutes.
2. Add the fish and cook it for 4 minutes on each side.
3. Add the rest of the ingredients, cook for 7 minutes more, divide between plates and serve.

Nutrition info per serving: calories 232, fat 12.3, fiber 4, carbs 8.7, protein 12

Salmon and Mango

Prep time: 5 minutes I **Cooking time:** 0 minutes I **Servings:** 4

Ingredients:
- 1 pound smoked salmon, boneless, skinless and flaked
- Black pepper to the taste
- 1 red onion, chopped
- 1 mango, peeled, seedless and chopped
- 2 jalapeno peppers, chopped
- ¼ cup parsley, chopped
- 3 tablespoons lime juice
- 1 tablespoon olive oil

Directions:
2. In a bowl, mix the salmon with the black pepper and the other ingredients, toss and serve.

Nutrition info per serving: calories 323, fat 14.2, fiber 4, carbs 8.5, protein 20.4

Shrimp and Radish Mix

Prep time: 5 minutes I **Cooking time:** 0 minutes I **Servings:** 4

Ingredients:
- 2 teaspoons lemon juice
- 1 tablespoon olive oil
- 1 tablespoon dill, chopped
- 1 pound shrimp, cooked, peeled and deveined
- Black pepper to the taste
- 1 cup radishes, cubed

Directions:
1. In a bowl, combine the shrimp with the lemon juice and the other ingredients, toss and serve.

Nutrition info per serving: calories 292, fat 13, fiber 4.4, carbs 8, protein 16.4

Cheesy Salmon Spread

Prep time: 4 minutes I **Cooking time:** 0 minutes I **Servings:** 6

Ingredients:
- 6 ounces smoked salmon, boneless, skinless and shredded
- 2 tablespoons non-fat yogurt
- 3 teaspoons lemon juice
- 2 spring onions, chopped
- 8 ounces cream cheese
- ¼ cup cilantro, chopped

Directions:
1. In a bowl, mix the salmon with the yogurt and the other ingredients, whisk and serve cold.

Nutrition info per serving: calories 272, fat 15.2, fiber 4.3, carbs 16.8, protein 9.9

Shrimp with Artichokes and Tomatoes

Prep time: 4 minutes I **Cooking time:** 8 minutes I **Servings:** 4

Ingredients:
- 2 green onions, chopped
- 1 cup artichokes, quartered
- 2 tablespoons cilantro, chopped
- 1 pound shrimp, peeled and deveined
- 1 cup cherry tomatoes, cubed
- 1 tablespoon olive oil
- 1 tablespoon balsamic vinegar
- A pinch of salt and black pepper

Directions:
1. Heat up a pan with the oil over medium heat, add the onions and the artichokes, toss and cook for 2 minutes.
2. Add the shrimp, toss and cook over medium heat for 6 minutes.
3. Divide everything into bowls and serve.

Nutrition info per serving: calories 260, fat 8.23, fiber 3.8, carbs 14.3, protein 12.4

Shrimp and Sauce

Prep time: 5 minutes I **Cooking time:** 8 minutes I **Servings:** 4

Ingredients:
- 1 pound shrimp, peeled and deveined
- 2 tablespoons olive oil
- Zest of 1 lemon, grated
- Juice of ½ lemon
- 1 tablespoon chives, chopped

Directions:
1. Heat up a pan with the oil over medium-high heat, add the lemon zest, lemon juice and the cilantro, toss and cook for 2 minutes.
2. Add the shrimp, cook everything for 6 minutes more, divide between plates and serve.

Nutrition info per serving: calories 195, fat 8.9, fiber 0, carbs 1.8, protein 25.9

Oregano Tuna and Orange

Prep time: 5 minutes I **Cooking time:** 12 minutes I **Servings:** 4

Ingredients:
- 4 tuna fillets, boneless
- Black pepper to the taste
- 2 tablespoons olive oil
- 2 shallots, chopped
- 3 tablespoons orange juice
- 1 orange, peeled and cut into segments
- 1 tablespoon oregano, chopped

Directions:
1. Heat up a pan with the oil over medium-high heat, add the shallots, stir and sauté for 2 minutes.
2. Add the tuna and the other ingredients, cook everything for 10 minutes more, divide between plates and serve.

Nutrition info per serving: calories 457, fat 38.2, fiber 1.6, carbs 8.2, protein 21.8

Fish Curry

Prep time: 10 minutes I **Cooking time:** 20 minutes I **Servings:** 4

Ingredients:
- 1 pound salmon fillet, boneless and cubed
- 3 tablespoons red curry paste
- 1 red onion, chopped
- 1 teaspoon sweet paprika
- 1 cup coconut cream
- 1 tablespoon olive oil
- Black pepper to the taste
- ½ cup chicken stock
- 3 tablespoons basil, chopped

Directions:
1. Heat up a pan with the oil over medium-high heat, add the onion, paprika and the curry paste, toss and cook for 5 minutes.
2. Add the salmon and the other ingredients, toss gently, cook over medium heat for 15 minutes, divide into bowls and serve.

Nutrition info per serving: calories 377, fat 28.3, fiber 2.1, carbs 8.5, protein 23.9

Salmon and Carrots Mix

Prep time: 10 minutes I **Cooking time:** 15 minutes I **Servings:** 4

Ingredients:
- 4 salmon fillets, boneless
- 1 red onion, chopped
- 2 carrots, sliced
- 2 tablespoons olive oil
- 2 tablespoons balsamic vinegar
- Black pepper to the taste
- 2 tablespoons chives, chopped
- ¼ cup veggie stock

Directions:
1. Heat up a pan with the oil over medium heat, add the onion and the carrots, toss and sauté for 5 minutes.
2. Add the salmon and the other ingredients, cook everything for 10 minutes more, divide between plates and serve.

Nutrition info per serving: calories 322, fat 18, fiber 1.4, carbs 6, protein 35.2

Thyme Shrimp

Prep time: 10 minutes I **Cooking time:** 10 minutes I **Servings:** 4

Ingredients:
- 1 pound shrimp, peeled and deveined
- 2 tablespoons pine nuts
- 1 tablespoon lime juice
- 2 tablespoons olive oil
- 3 garlic cloves, minced
- Black pepper to the taste
- 1 tablespoon thyme, chopped
- 2 tablespoons chives, finely chopped

Directions:
1. Heat up a pan with the oil over medium-high heat, add the garlic, thyme, pine nuts and lime juice, toss and cook for 3 minutes.
2. Add the shrimp, black pepper and the chives, toss, cook for 7 minutes more, divide between plates and serve.

Nutrition info per serving: calories 290, fat 13, fiber 4.5, carbs 13.9, protein 10

Chili Cumin Cod

Prep time: 10 minutes I **Cooking time:** 14 minutes I **Servings:** 4

Ingredients:
- 4 cod fillets, boneless
- ½ pound green beans, trimmed and halved
- 1 tablespoon lime juice
- 1 tablespoon lime zest, grated
- 1 yellow onion, chopped
- 2 tablespoons olive oil
- 1 teaspoon cumin, ground
- 1 teaspoon chili powder
- ½ cup veggie stock
- A pinch of salt and black pepper

Directions:
1. Heat up a pan with the oil over medium-high heat, add the onion, toss and cook for 2 minutes.
2. Add the fish and cook it for 3 minutes on each side.
3. Add the green beans and the rest of the ingredients, toss gently, cook for 7 minutes more, divide between plates and serve.

Nutrition info per serving: calories 220, fat 13, carbs 14.3, fiber 2.3, protein 12

Balsamic Scallops

Prep time: 5 minutes I **Cooking time:** 8 minutes I **Servings:** 4

Ingredients:
- 12 scallops
- 1 red onion, sliced
- 2 tablespoons olive oil
- ½ teaspoon garlic, minced
- 2 tablespoons lemon juice
- Black pepper to the taste
- 1 teaspoon balsamic vinegar

Directions:
1. Heat up a pan with the oil over medium heat, add the onion and the garlic and sauté for 2 minutes.
2. Add the scallops and the other ingredients, cook over medium heat for 6 minutes more, divide between plates and serve hot.

Nutrition info per serving: calories 259, fat 8, fiber 3, carbs 5.7, protein 7

Creamy Lime Sea Bass Mix

Prep time: 10 minutes I **Cooking time:** 14 minutes I **Servings:** 4

Ingredients:
- 4 sea bass fillets, boneless
- 1 cup coconut cream
- 1 yellow onion, chopped
- 1 tablespoon lime juice
- 2 tablespoons avocado oil
- 1 tablespoon parsley, chopped
- A pinch of black pepper

Directions:
1. Heat up a pan with the oil over medium heat, add the onion, toss and sauté for 2 minutes.
2. Add the fish and cook it for 4 minutes on each side.
3. Add the rest of the ingredients, cook everything for 4 minutes more, divide between plates and serve.

Nutrition info per serving: calories 283, fat 12.3, fiber 5, carbs 12.5, protein 8

Fish and Mushrooms Mix

Prep time: 10 minutes I **Cooking time:** 13 minutes I **Servings:** 4

Ingredients:
- 4 sea bass fillets, boneless
- 2 tablespoons olive oil
- Black pepper to the taste
- ½ cup white mushrooms, sliced
- 1 red onion, chopped
- 2 tablespoons balsamic vinegar
- 3 tablespoons cilantro, chopped

Directions:
1. Heat up a pan with the oil over medium-high heat, add the onion and the mushrooms, stir and cook for 5 minutes.
2. Add the fish and the other ingredients, cook for 4 minutes on each side, divide everything between plates and serve.

Nutrition info per serving: calories 280, fat 12.3, fiber 8, carbs 13.6, protein 14.3

Salmon and Tomato Soup

Prep time: 5 minutes I **Cooking time:** 20 minutes I **Servings:** 4

Ingredients:
- 1 pound salmon fillets, boneless, skinless and cubed
- 1 cup yellow onion, chopped
- 2 tablespoons olive oil
- Black pepper to the taste
- 2 cups veggie stock
- 1 and ½ cups tomatoes, chopped
- 1 tablespoon basil, chopped

Directions:
1. Heat up a pot with the oil over medium heat, add the onion, stir and sauté for 5 minutes.
2. Add the salmon and the other ingredients, bring to a simmer and cook over medium heat for 15 minutes.
3. Divide the chowder into bowls and serve.

Nutrition info per serving: calories 250, fat 12.2, fiber 5, carbs 8.5, protein 7

Cinnamon Shrimp

Prep time: 3 minutes I **Cooking time:** 6 minutes I **Servings:** 4

Ingredients:
- 1 pound shrimp, peeled and deveined
- 2 tablespoons olive oil
- 1 tablespoon lemon juice
- 1 tablespoon cinnamon, ground
- Black pepper to the taste
- 1 tablespoon cilantro, chopped

Directions:
1. Heat up a pan with the oil over medium heat, add the shrimp, lemon juice and the other ingredients, toss, cook for 6 minutes, divide into bowls and serve.

Nutrition info per serving: calories 205, fat 9.6, fiber 0.4, carbs 2.7, protein 26

Shrimp and Blueberries Mix

Prep time: 4 minutes I **Cooking time:** 6 minutes I **Servings:** 4

Ingredients:
- 1 pound shrimp, peeled and deveined
- ½ cup tomatoes, cubed
- 2 tablespoons olive oil
- 1 tablespoon balsamic vinegar
- ½ cup blueberries, chopped
- Black pepper to the taste

Directions:
1. Heat up a pan with the oil over medium heat, add the shrimp, toss and cook for 3 minutes.
2. Add the rest of the ingredients, toss, cook for 3-4 minutes more, divide into bowls and serve.

Nutrition info per serving: calories 205, fat 9, fiber 0.6, carbs 4, protein 26.2

Baked Trout

Prep time: 10 minutes I **Cooking time:** 30 minutes I **Servings:** 4

Ingredients:
- 4 trout
- 1 tablespoon lemon zest, grated
- 2 tablespoons olive oil
- 2 tablespoons lemon juice
- A pinch of black pepper
- 2 tablespoons cilantro, chopped

Directions:
1. In a baking dish, combine the fish with the lemon zest and the other ingredients and rub.
2. Bake at 370 degrees F for 30 minutes, divide between plates and serve.

Nutrition info per serving: calories 264, fat 12.3, fiber 5, carbs 7, protein 11

Paprika Scallops

Prep time: 3 minutes I **Cooking time:** 4 minutes I **Servings:** 4

Ingredients:
- 12 scallops
- 2 tablespoons olive oil
- Black pepper to the taste
- 2 tablespoons chives, chopped
- 1 tablespoon sweet paprika

Directions:
1. Heat up a pan with the oil over medium heat, add the scallops, paprika and the other ingredients, and cook for 2 minutes on each side.
2. Divide between plates and serve with a side salad.

Nutrition info per serving: calories 215, fat 6, fiber 5, carbs 4.5, protein 11

Fish Meatballs

Prep time: 10 minutes I **Cooking time:** 30 minutes I **Servings:** 4

Ingredients:
- 2 tablespoons olive oil
- 1 pound tuna, skinless, boneless and minced
- 1 yellow onion, chopped
- ¼ cup chives, chopped
- 1 egg, whisked
- 1 tablespoon coconut flour
- A pinch of salt and black pepper

Directions:
1. In a bowl, mix the tuna with the onion and the other ingredients except the oil, stir well and shape medium meatballs out of this mix.
2. Arrange the meatballs on a baking sheet, grease them with the oil, introduce in the oven at 350 degrees F, cook for 30 minutes, divide between plates and serve.

Nutrition info per serving: calories 291, fat 14.3, fiber 5, carbs 12.4, protein 11

Salmon and Eggplant Pan

Prep time: 10 minutes I **Cooking time:** 12 minutes I **Servings:** 4

Ingredients:
- 4 salmon fillets, boneless and roughly cubed
- 2 tablespoons olive oil
- 1 red bell pepper, cut into strips
- 2 eggplants, roughly cubed
- 1 tablespoon lemon juice
- 1 tablespoon dill, chopped
- ¼ cup veggie stock
- 1 teaspoon garlic powder
- A pinch of black pepper

Directions:
1. Heat up a pan with oil over medium-high heat, add the bell pepper and the eggplant, toss and sauté for 3 minutes.
2. Add the salmon and the other ingredients, toss gently, cook everything for 9 minutes more, divide between plates and serve.

Nutrition info per serving: calories 348, fat 18.4, fiber 5.3, carbs 11.9, protein 36.9

Mustard and Turmeric Cod

Prep time: 10 minutes I **Cooking time:** 25 minutes I **Servings:** 4

Ingredients:
- 4 cod fillets, skinless and boneless
- A pinch of black pepper
- 1 teaspoon ginger, grated
- 1 tablespoon mustard
- 2 tablespoons olive oil
- 1 teaspoon thyme, dried
- ¼ teaspoon cumin, ground
- 1 teaspoon turmeric powder
- ¼ cup cilantro, chopped
- 1 cup veggie stock
- 3 garlic cloves, minced

Directions:
1. In a roasting pan, combine the cod with the black pepper, ginger and the other ingredients, toss gently and bake at 380 degrees F for 25 minutes.
2. Divide the mix between plates and serve.

Nutrition info per serving: calories 176, fat 9, fiber 1, carbs 3.7, protein 21.2

Shrimp and Walnuts

Prep time: 10 minutes I **Cooking time:** 14 minutes I **Servings:** 4

Ingredients:
- 1/2 cup walnuts, chopped
- 1 pound shrimp, peeled and deveined
- Black pepper to the taste
- 2 tablespoons olive oil
- 1 red onion, chopped
- 2 garlic cloves, minced
- 1 cup coconut cream

Directions:
1. Heat up a pan with the oil over medium heat, add the onion, garlic and the walnuts, toss and cook for 4 minutes.
2. Add the shrimp and the other ingredients, toss, simmer over medium heat for 10 minutes, divide everything into bowls and serve.

Nutrition info per serving: calories 225, fat 6, fiber 3.4, carbs 8.6, protein 8

Cod and Corn

Prep time: 10 minutes I **Cooking time:** 20 minutes I **Servings:** 4

Ingredients:
- 1 yellow onion, chopped
- 2 tablespoons olive oil
- ½ cup chicken stock
- 4 cod fillets, boneless, skinless
- Black pepper to the taste
- 1 cup corn

Directions:
1. Heat up a pot with the oil over medium heat, add the onion, stir and sauté fro 4 minutes.
2. Add the fish and cook it for 3 minutes on each side.
3. Add the corn and the other ingredients, cook everything for 10 minutes more, divide between plates and serve.

Nutrition info per serving: calories 240, fat 8.4, fiber 2.7, carbs 7.6, protein 14

Shrimp and Mussels Mix

Prep time: 5 minutes I **Cooking time:** 12 minutes I **Servings:** 4

Ingredients:
- 1 pound mussels, scrubbed
- ½ cup chicken stock
- 1 pound shrimp, peeled and deveined
- 2 shallots, minced
- 1 cup cherry tomatoes, cubed
- 2 garlic cloves, minced
- 1 tablespoon olive oil
- Juice of 1 lemon

Directions:
1. Heat up a pan with the oil over medium heat, add the shallots and the garlic and sauté for 2 minutes.
2. Add the shrimp, mussels and the other ingredients, cook everything over medium heat for 10 minutes, divide into bowls and serve.

Nutrition info per serving: calories 240, fat 4.9, fiber 2.4, carbs 11.6, protein 8

Walnuts Salmon

Prep time: 10 minutes I **Cooking time:** 20 minutes I **Servings:** 4

Ingredients:
- 4 salmon fillets, boneless
- 2 tablespoons olive oil
- 2 tablespoons walnuts, chopped
- 1 tablespoon parsley, chopped
- 2 tablespoons vegetable stock
- 1 teaspoon rosemary, dried
- Salt and black pepper to the taste

Directions:
1. In a roasting pan, combine the salmon with the oil, the walnuts and the other ingredients, toss gently and cook at 380 degrees F for 20 minutes.
2. Divide the mix between plates and serve with a side salad.

Nutrition info per serving: calories 323, fat 20.9, fiber 0.4, carbs 1.1, protein 35.5

Salmon with Brussels Sprouts

Prep time: 5 minutes I **Cooking time:** 20 minutes I **Servings:** 4

Ingredients:
- 2 tablespoons avocado oil
- 1 cup brussels sprouts
- 4 salmon fillets, skinless
- 1 teaspoon chili powder
- 1 teaspoon cumin, ground
- 1 tablespoon chives, chopped
- A pinch of sea salt and black pepper

Directions:
1. In a baking dish, combine the salmon fillets with the oil, the broccoli and the other ingredients, toss gently and cook at 380 degrees F for 20 minutes.
2. Divide everything between plates and serve.

Nutrition info per serving: calories 257, fat 12.2, fiber 1.2, carbs 2.5, protein 35.5

Salmon with Ginger

Prep time: 10 minutes I **Cooking time:** 20 minutes I **Servings:** 4

Ingredients:
- 4 salmon fillets, boneless
- 4 scallions, chopped
- 2 tablespoons avocado oil
- 2 garlic cloves, minced
- 1 tablespoon ginger, grated
- 1 teaspoon turmeric powder
- 1 teaspoon rosemary, dried
- 1 tablespoon parsley, chopped

Directions:
1. Heat up a pan with the oil over medium heat, add the scallions, garlic and ginger and sauté for 5 minutes.
2. Add the fish and the other ingredients, cook for 15 minutes more, flipping the fish halfway, divide between plates and serve.

Nutrition info per serving: calories 260, fat 12.1, fiber 1.2, carbs 3.6, protein 35.2

Cilantro Trout and Olives

Prep time: 10 minutes I **Cooking time:** 30 minutes I **Servings:** 4

Ingredients:
- 4 trout fillets, boneless
- 1 cup green olives, pitted
- 2 tablespoons olive oil
- ½ teaspoon smoked paprika
- ½ teaspoon cumin, ground
- Salt and black pepper to the taste
- ¼ cup vegetable stock
- 2 tablespoons cilantro, chopped

Directions:
1. In a roasting pan, combine the trout fillets with the olives, the oil and the other ingredients, toss gently and cook at 380 degrees F for 30 minutes.
2. Divide the mix between plates and serve.

Nutrition info per serving: calories 191, fat 13.6, fiber 0.4, carbs 1.4, protein 16.7

Salmon with Rice

Prep time: 5 minutes I **Cooking time:** 20 minutes I **Servings:** 4

Ingredients:
- 4 salmon fillets, boneless and cubed
- ½ cup snow peas, blanched
- 1 cup black rice, cooked
- 2 tablespoons olive oil
- Salt and pepper to the taste
- 4 scallions, chopped
- 1 red chili, chopped
- Juice of 1 lime
- 1 tablespoon chives, chopped

Directions:
1. Heat up a pan with the oil over medium heat, add the chili and the scallions and sauté for 5 minutes.
2. Add the fish and cook it for 5 minutes more.
3. Add the peas, rice and the remaining ingredients, toss, cook over medium heat for 10 more minutes, divide into bowls and serve.

Nutrition info per serving: calories 354, fat 18.8, fiber 2, carbs 10.5, protein 37.5

Chives and Chili Salmon

Prep time: 5 minutes I **Cooking time:** 15 minutes I **Servings:** 4

Ingredients:
- 4 salmon fillets, boneless
- 1 teaspoon chili powder
- 1 teaspoon hot paprika
- 2 tablespoons olive oil
- 2 spring onions, chopped
- A pinch of salt and black pepper
- ¼ cup fresh chives, chopped
- 1 tablespoon lemon juice

Directions:
1. Heat up a pan with the oil over medium heat, add the spring onions and sauté for 2 minutes.
2. Add the fish and cook it for 5 minutes on each side.
3. Add the rest of the ingredients, toss gently, cook for 3 minutes more, divide everything between plates and serve.

Nutrition info per serving: calories 272, fat 4, fiber 2, carbs 12, protein 7

Coconut and Parsley Salmon

Prep time: 5 minutes I **Cooking time:** 14 minutes I **Servings:** 4

Ingredients:
- 1 cup coconut cream
- 4 salmon fillets, boneless
- 2 tablespoons avocado oil
- 4 scallions, chopped
- 1 tablespoon parsley, chopped
- 1 tablespoon lemon juice
- A pinch of salt and black pepper

Directions:
1. Heat up a pan with the oil over medium-high heat, add the scallions and sauté for 4 minutes.
2. Add the fish and cook it for 3 minutes on each side.
3. Add the rest of the ingredients, toss gently, cook for 4 minutes more, divide between plates and serve.

Nutrition info per serving: calories 215, fat 3, fiber 2, carbs 8, protein 6

Smoked Trout and Avocado Bowls

Prep time: 10 minutes I **Cooking time:** 0 minutes I **Servings:** 4

Ingredients:
- 1 pound smoked trout, boneless, skinless and flaked
- 1 cup baby arugula
- 2 tablespoons lemon juice
- 2 tomatoes, cubed
- 1 avocado, peeled, pitted and cubed
- 1 tablespoon chives, minced
- 1 tablespoon olive oil
- A pinch of salt and black pepper

Directions:
1. In a bowl, mix the trout with the arugula and the other ingredients, toss and serve.

Nutrition info per serving: calories 200, fat 7, fiber 3, carbs 12, protein 6

Shrimp, Onion and Spinach Salad

Prep time: 5 minutes I **Cooking time:** 0 minutes I **Servings:** 4

Ingredients:
- 3 tablespoons balsamic vinegar
- 2 tablespoons olive oil
- 2 garlic cloves, minced
- A pinch of salt and black pepper
- 1 pound shrimp, cooked, peeled and deveined
- ½ pound cherry tomatoes, halved
- ½ red onion, sliced
- 1 cup baby spinach

Directions:
1. In a bowl, combine the shrimp with the tomatoes, the spinach and the other ingredients, toss and serve.

Nutrition info per serving: calories 212, fat 7.3, fiber 3, carbs 6, protein 7

Saffron Cloves Shrimp

Prep time: 5 minutes I **Cooking time:** 8 minutes I **Servings:** 4

Ingredients:
- 1 pound shrimp, peeled and deveined
- 1 tablespoon lemon juice
- ½ teaspoon sweet paprika
- 2 tablespoons olive oil
- 1 teaspoon saffron powder
- 1 teaspoon coriander, ground
- 1 teaspoon orange zest, grated
- ½ teaspoon cloves, ground
- 1 tablespoon cilantro, chopped

Directions:
1. Heat up a pan with the oil over medium heat, add the shrimp, lemon juice, saffron and the other ingredients, toss, cook for 8 minutes, divide the mix intro bowls and serve.

Nutrition info per serving: calories 230, fat 6.2, fiber 5, carbs 8, protein 4

Salmon and Rosemary Mix

Prep time: 5 minutes I **Cooking time:** 14 minutes I **Servings:** 4

Ingredients:
- 4 salmon fillets, boneless
- A pinch of salt and black pepper
- Juice of 1 lime
- 1 fennel bulb, sliced
- 2 tablespoons olive oil
- ½ teaspoon fennel seeds, crushed
- 1 teaspoon rosemary, dried
- 1 tablespoon cilantro, chopped

Directions:
1. Heat up a pan with the oil over medium-high heat, add the fennel and sauté for 2 minutes.
2. Add the fish and the rest of the ingredients, cook it for 6 minutes on each side, divide between plates and serve.

Nutrition info per serving: calories 200, fat 2, fiber 4, carbs 10, protein 8

Shrimp and Coriander Tomatoes

Prep time: 5 minutes I **Cooking time:** 8 minutes I **Servings:** 4

Ingredients:
- 1 pound shrimp, peeled and deveined
- 2 tablespoons olive oil
- 1 cup tomatoes, cubed
- 1 tablespoon lime juice
- 3 garlic cloves, minced
- A pinch of salt and black pepper
- ¼ cup pine nuts, toasted
- 2 tablespoons coriander, ground

Directions:
1. Heat up a pan with the oil over medium-high heat, add the garlic and the pine nuts and cook for 2 minutes.
2. Add the shrimp and the other ingredients, toss, cook over medium heat for 6 minutes, divide into bowls and serve.

Nutrition info per serving: calories 211, fat 10, fiber 4, carbs 5, protein 14

Orange Shrimp

Prep time: 5 minutes I **Cooking time:** 8 minutes I **Servings:** 4

Ingredients:
- 2 pounds shrimp, peeled and deveined
- 2 scallions, chopped
- 1 orange, peeled and cut into segments
- 2 tablespoons olive oil
- ½ cup orange juice
- 1 tablespoon orange zest, grated
- 2 tablespoons chives, chopped

Directions:
1. Heat up a pan with the oil over medium heat, add the scallions, orange juice and zest and cook for 2 minutes.
2. Add the shrimp and the remaining ingredients, toss, cook for 6 minutes more, divide into bowls and serve.

Nutrition info per serving: calories 210, fat 6, fiber 4, carbs 8, protein 14

Trout with Scallions and Green Beans

Prep time: 5 minutes I **Cooking time:** 12 minutes I **Servings:** 4

Ingredients:

- 4 trout fillets, boneless
- 2 tablespoons olive oil
- 4 scallions, chopped
- 1 cup green beans, trimmed and halved
- 1 tablespoon lemon juice
- 2 tablespoons cilantro, chopped

Directions:

1. Heat up a pan with the oil over medium-high heat, add the scallions and sauté for 2 minutes.
2. Add the fish and the other ingredients, cook for 5 minutes on each side, divide everything between plates and serve.

Nutrition info per serving: calories 209, fat 9, fiber 6, carbs 8, protein 14

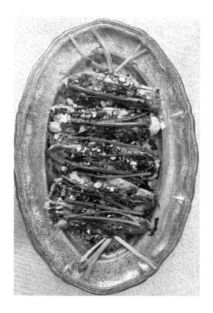

Cinnamon Cod

Prep time: 5 minutes I **Cooking time:** 12 minutes I **Servings:** 4

Ingredients:
- 4 cod fillets, boneless
- 2 tablespoons olive oil
- 1 tablespoon cinnamon powder
- ½ cup spring onions, chopped
- A pinch of salt and black pepper
- Juice of 1 lime

Directions:
1. Heat up a pan with the oil over medium heat, add the spring onions and sauté for 2 minutes.
2. Add the fish and the other ingredients, cook for 5 minutes on each side, divide between plates and serve.

Nutrition info per serving: calories 210, fat 12, fiber 4, carbs 7, protein 14

Salmon and Cantaloupe Salad

Prep time: 5 minutes I **Cooking time:** 0 minutes I **Servings:** 4

Ingredients:
- 2 cups smoked salmon, boneless and flaked
- 1 cup cantaloupe, peeled and cubed
- 2 tomatoes, cubed
- 1 cucumber, sliced
- 2 tablespoons olive oil
- 1 tablespoon lime juice
- Salt and black pepper to the taste

Directions:
1. In a salad bowl, combine the salmon with the cantaloupe, tomatoes and the other ingredients, toss and serve.

Nutrition info per serving: calories 169, fat 2, fiber 2, carbs 12, protein 17

Cayenne Sea Bass and Olives

Prep time: 5 minutes I **Cooking time:** 14 minutes I **Servings:** 4

Ingredients:
- 4 sea bass fillets, boneless
- 2 tablespoons avocado oil
- 4 scallions, chopped
- ½ cup corn
- ½ cup kalamata olives, pitted and cubed
- 1 teaspoon cayenne pepper
- Juice of ½ lemon
- A pinch of sea salt and black pepper
- 1/3 cup basil, chopped

Directions:
1. Heat up a pan with the oil over medium-high heat, add the scallions and sauté for 2 minutes.
2. Add the fish and cook it for 4 minutes on each side.
3. Add the rest of the ingredients, toss, cook for 4 minutes more, divide between plates and serve.

Nutrition info per serving: calories 270, fat 6, fiber 4, carbs 13, protein 15

Salmon with Leeks

Prep time: 10 minutes I **Cooking time:** 20 minutes I **Servings:** 4

Ingredients:
- 4 salmon fillets, boneless
- 2 tablespoons olive oil
- 2 leeks, sliced
- 1 teaspoon cumin, ground
- ½ teaspoon rosemary, dried
- 1 tablespoon ginger, grated
- 1 tablespoon cilantro, chopped
- 1 teaspoon sweet paprika

Directions:
1. Heat up a pan with the oil over medium heat, add the leeks and sauté for 5 minutes.
2. Add the fish and cook it for 5 minutes on each side.
3. Add the rest of the ingredients, cook the mix for 5 minutes more, divide between plates and serve.

Nutrition info per serving: calories 278, fat 3, fiber 4, carbs 14, protein 15

Curry and Coconut Halibut

Prep time: 10 minutes I **Cooking time:** 14 minutes I **Servings:** 4

Ingredients:
- 4 halibut fillets, boneless
- 2 tablespoons olive oil
- 4 shallots, chopped
- 1 tablespoon green curry paste
- ¼ cup basil, chopped
- 2 teaspoons coconut aminos
- 1 red chili pepper, chopped
- 1 tablespoon cilantro, chopped

Directions:
1. Heat up a pan with the oil over medium-high heat, add the shallots, curry paste and chili pepper and sauté for 4 minutes.
2. Add the fish and the other ingredients, cook it for 5 minutes on each side, divide between plates and serve.

Nutrition info per serving: calories 210, fat 3, fiber 2, carbs 12, protein 16

Salmon and Rosemary Sweet Potatoes

Prep time: 10 minutes I **Cooking time:** 25 minutes I **Servings:** 4

Ingredients:
- 4 salmon fillets, boneless
- 1 garlic cloves, minced
- 2 tablespoons olive oil
- A pinch of salt and black pepper
- 1 yellow onion, sliced
- 2 sweet potatoes, peeled and cut into wedges
- 1 tablespoon rosemary, chopped
- 1 tablespoon lime juice

Directions:
1. Grease a baking dish with the oil, arrange the salmon, garlic, onion and the other ingredients into the dish and bake everything at 380 degrees F for 25 minutes.
2. Divide the mix between plates and serve.

Nutrition info per serving: calories 260, fat 4, fiber 6, carbs 10, protein 16

Salmon with Herbs

Prep time: 5 minutes I **Cooking time:** 20 minutes I **Servings:** 4

Ingredients:
- 3 tablespoons olive oil
- 4 salmon fillets, boneless
- 4 garlic cloves, minced
- ¼ cup coconut cream
- 1 tablespoon parsley, chopped
- 1 tablespoon rosemary, chopped
- 1 tablespoon basil, chopped
- 1 tablespoon oregano, chopped
- 1 tablespoon pine nuts, toasted
- A pinch of salt and black pepper

Directions:
1. In a blender, combine the oil with the garlic and the other ingredients except the fish and pulse well.
2. Arrange the fish in a roasting pan, add the herbed sauce on top and cook at 380 degrees F for 20 minutes.
3. Divide the mix between plates and serve.

Nutrition info per serving: calories 386, fat 26.8, fiber 1.4, carbs 3.5, protein 35.6

Shrimp and Pinto Beans

Prep time: 5 minutes I **Cooking time:** 12 minutes I **Servings:** 4

Ingredients:
- 1 pound shrimp, peeled and deveined
- 2 tablespoons olive oil
- 1 teaspoon cumin, ground
- 4 green onions, chopped
- 1 cup pinto beans, cooked
- 2 tablespoons lime juice
- 1 teaspoon turmeric powder

Directions:
1. Heat up a pan with the oil over medium heat, add the green onions and sauté for 2 minutes.
2. Add the shrimp and the other ingredients, toss, cook over medium heat for another 10 minutes, divide between plates and serve.

Nutrition info per serving: calories 251, fat 12, fiber 2, carbs 13, protein 16

Shrimp with Baby Spinach

Prep time: 10 minutes I **Cooking time:** 10 minutes I **Servings:** 4

Ingredients:
- 1 pound shrimp, peeled and deveined
- 2 tablespoons olive oil
- 1 tablespoon lime juice
- 1 cup baby spinach
- A pinch of sea salt and black pepper
- 1 tablespoon chives, chopped

Directions:
1. Heat up the pan with the oil over medium heat, add the shrimp and sauté for 5 minutes.
2. Add the spinach and the remaining ingredients, toss, cook the mix for another 5 minutes, divide between plates and serve.

Nutrition info per serving: calories 206, fat 6, fiber 4, carbs 7, protein 17

Cod and Peppers

Prep time: 10 minutes I **Cooking time:** 15 minutes I **Servings:** 4

Ingredients:
- 4 cod fillets, boneless
- 2 tablespoons olive oil
- 4 spring onions, chopped
- Juice of 1 lime
- 1 red bell pepper, cut into strips
- 1 green bell pepper, cut into strips
- 2 teaspoons parsley, chopped
- A pinch of salt and black pepper

Directions:
1. Heat up a pan with the oil over medium heat, add the bell peppers and the onions and sauté for 5 minutes.
2. Add the fish and the rest of the ingredients, cook the mix for 10 minutes more, flipping the fish halfway.
3. Divide the mix between plates and serve.

Nutrition info per serving: calories 180, fat 5, fiber 1, carbs 7, protein 11

Cod with Avocado and Peppers Pan

Prep time: 5 minutes I **Cooking time:** 20 minutes I **Servings:** 4

Ingredients:
- 1 pound cod fillets, boneless and cubed
- 2 tablespoons avocado oil
- 1 avocado, peeled, pitted and cubed
- 1 red sweet pepper, cut into strips
- 1 tablespoon lemon juice
- ¼ cup parsley, chopped
- 1 tablespoon tomato paste
- ½ cup veggie stock
- A pinch of sea salt and black pepper

Directions:
1. Heat up a pan with the oil over medium-high heat, add the fish and cook for 3 minutes on each side.
2. Add the rest of the ingredients, cook the mix for 14 minutes more over medium heat, divide between plates and serve.

Nutrition info per serving: calories 160, fat 2, fiber 2, carbs 4, protein 7

Shrimp and Zucchinis

Prep time: 5 minutes I **Cooking time:** 8 minutes I **Servings:** 4

Ingredients:
- 1 pound shrimp, peeled and deveined
- 2 tablespoons avocado oil
- 2 zucchinis, sliced
- Juice of 1 lime
- A pinch of salt and black pepper
- 2 red chilies, chopped
- 3 garlic cloves, minced
- 1 tablespoon balsamic vinegar

Directions:
1. Heat up a pan with the oil over medium-high heat, add the shrimp, garlic and the chilies and cook for 3 minutes.
2. Add the rest of the ingredients, toss, cook everything for 5 minutes more, divide between plates and serve.

Nutrition info per serving: calories 211, fat 5, fiber 2, carbs 11, protein 15

Lemon Rosemary Scallops

Prep time: 10 minutes I **Cooking time:** 10 minutes I **Servings:** 4

Ingredients:
- 2 tablespoons olive oil
- 1 pound sea scallops
- ½ teaspoon rosemary, dried
- ½ cup veggie stock
- 2 garlic cloves, minced
- Juice of ½ lemon

Directions:
1. Heat up a pan with the oil over medium-high heat, add the garlic, the scallops and the other ingredients, cook everything for 10 minutes, divide into bowls and serve.

Nutrition info per serving: calories 170, fat 5, fiber 2, carbs 8, protein 10

Crab and Kale Salad

Prep time: 5 minutes I **Cooking time:** 0 minutes I **Servings:** 4

Ingredients:
- 1 cup crab meat, cooked
- 1 pound shrimp, peeled, deveined and cooked
- 1 cup cherry tomatoes, halved
- 1 cucumber, sliced
- 2 cups baby kale
- 2 tablespoons avocado oil
- 1 tablespoon chives, chopped
- 1 tablespoon lemon juice
- A pinch of salt and black pepper

Directions:
1. In a bowl, combine the shrimp with the crab meat and the other ingredients, toss and serve.

Nutrition info per serving: calories 203, fat 12, fiber 6, carbs 12, protein 9

Salmon with Paprika Tomatoes

Prep time: 10 minutes I **Cooking time:** 30 minutes I **Servings:** 4

Ingredients:
- 4 salmon fillets, boneless
- 2 tablespoons avocado oil
- 2 tablespoons sweet paprika
- 2 tomatoes, cut into wedges
- ¼ teaspoon red pepper flakes, crushed
- A pinch of sea salt and black pepper
- 4 garlic cloves, minced

Directions:
1. In a roasting pan, combine the salmon with the oil and the other ingredients, toss gently and cook at 370 degrees F for 30 minutes.
2. Divide everything between plates and serve.

Nutrition info per serving: calories 210, fat 2, fiber 4, carbs 13, protein 10

Shrimp and Mango Salad

Prep time: 5 minutes I **Cooking time:** 0 minutes I **Servings:** 4

Ingredients:
- 1 pound shrimp, cooked, peeled and deveined
- 2 mangoes, peeled and cubed
- 3 scallions, chopped
- 1 cup baby spinach
- 1 cup baby arugula
- 1 jalapeno, chopped
- 2 tablespoons olive oil
- 1 tablespoon lime juice
- A pinch of salt and black pepper

Directions:
1. In a bowl, combine the shrimp with the mango, scallions and the other ingredients, toss and serve.

Nutrition info per serving: calories 210, fat 2, fiber 3, carbs 13, protein 8

Creamy Cod

Prep time: 5 minutes I **Cooking time:** 20 minutes I **Servings:** 4

Ingredients:
- 2 tablespoons olive oil
- 1 pound cod fillets, boneless and cubed
- 2 spring onions, chopped
- 2 garlic cloves, minced
- 1 cup coconut cream
- ¼ cup chives, chopped
- A pinch of salt and black pepper
- 2 tablespoons Dijon mustard

Directions:
1. Heat up a pan with the oil over medium heat, add the garlic and the onions and sauté for 5 minutes.
2. Add the fish and the other ingredients, toss, cook over medium heat for 15 minutes more, divide into bowls and serve.

Nutrition info per serving: calories 211, fat 5, fiber 5, carbs 6, protein 15

Trout and Walnuts Cilantro Sauce

Prep time: 5 minutes I **Cooking time:** 15 minutes I **Servings:** 4

Ingredients:
- 4 trout fillets, boneless
- 2 tablespoons avocado oil
- 1 cup cilantro, chopped
- 2 tablespoons lemon juice
- ½ cup coconut cream
- 1 tablespoon walnuts, chopped
- A pinch of salt and black pepper
- 3 teaspoons lemon zest, grated

Directions:
1. In a blender, combine the cilantro with the cream and the other ingredients except the fish and the oil and pulse well.
2. Heat up a pan with the oil over medium heat, add the fish and cook for 4 minutes on each side.
3. Add the cilantro sauce, toss gently and cook over medium heat for 7 minutes more.
4. Divide the mix between plates and serve.

Nutrition info per serving: calories 212, fat 14.6, fiber 1.3, carbs 2.9, protein 18

Cilantro Tilapia

Prep time: 5 minutes I **Cooking time:** 12 minutes I **Servings:** 4

Ingredients:
- 4 tilapia fillets, boneless
- 2 tablespoons olive oil
- 2 tablespoons lemon juice
- 1 teaspoon basil, dried
- 1 tablespoon cilantro, chopped

Directions:
1. Heat up a pan with the oil over medium heat, add the fish and cook for 5 minutes on each side.
2. Add the rest of the ingredients, toss gently, cook for 2 minutes more, divide between plates and serve.

Nutrition info per serving: calories 201, fat 8.6, fiber 0, carbs 0.2, protein 31.6

Salmon and Green Chilies Mix

Prep time: 5 minutes I **Cooking time:** 14 minutes I **Servings:** 4

Ingredients:
- 4 salmon fillets, boneless
- ½ teaspoon mustard seeds
- ½ cup mustard
- 2 tablespoons olive oil
- 4 scallions, chopped
- Salt and black pepper to the taste
- 2 green chilies, chopped
- ¼ teaspoon cumin, ground
- ¼ cup parsley, chopped

Directions:
1. Heat up a pot with the oil over medium heat, add the scallions and the chilies and cook for 2 minutes.
2. Add the fish and cook for 4 minutes on each side.
3. Add the remaining ingredients, toss, cook everything for 4 more minutes, divide between plates and serve.

Nutrition info per serving: calories 397, fat 23.9, fiber 3.5, carbs 8,5, protein 40

Salmon and Green Chilies Mix

Prep time: 5 minutes I **Cooking time:** 14 minutes I **Servings:** 4

Ingredients:
- 4 salmon fillets, boneless
- ½ teaspoon mustard seeds
- ½ cup mustard
- 2 tablespoons olive oil
- 4 scallions, chopped
- Salt and black pepper to the taste
- 2 green chilies, chopped
- ¼ teaspoon cumin, ground
- ¼ cup parsley, chopped

Directions:
3. Heat up a pot with the oil over medium heat, add the scallions and the chilies and cook for 2 minutes.
4. Add the fish and cook for 4 minutes on each side.
5. Add the remaining ingredients, toss, cook everything for 4 more minutes, divide between plates and serve.

Nutrition info per serving: calories 397, fat 23.9, fiber 3.5, carbs 8,5, protein 40

Shrimp and Turmeric Cauliflower Mix

Prep time: 10 minutes I **Cooking time:** 10 minutes I **Servings:** 4

Ingredients:
- 2 tablespoons olive oil
- 1 pound shrimp, peeled and deveined
- 1 cup cauliflower florets
- 2 tablespoons lemon juice
- 2 tablespoons garlic, minced
- 1 teaspoon cumin, ground
- 1 teaspoon turmeric powder
- Salt and black pepper to the taste

Directions:
1. Heat up a pan with the oil over medium-high heat, add the garlic and sauté for 2 minutes.
2. Add the shrimp and cook for 4 minutes more.
3. Add the remaining ingredients, toss, cook the mix for 4 minutes, divide between plates and serve

Nutrition info per serving: calories 200, fat 5.3, fiber 3, carbs 11, protein 6

Tuna with Broccoli

Prep time: 5 minutes I **Cooking time:** 15 minutes I **Servings:** 4

Ingredients:
- 4 tuna fillets, boneless
- 1 teaspoon coriander, ground
- 1 cup broccoli florets
- 2 tablespoons lemon juice
- 2 tablespoons avocado oil
- 1 tablespoon lemon zest, grated
- A pinch of salt and black pepper
- 2 tablespoons cilantro, chopped

Directions:
1. Heat up a pan with the oil over medium heat, add the fish and cook for 4 minutes on each side.
2. Add the broccoli and the other ingredients, cook the mix for 7 more minutes, divide between plates and serve.

Nutrition info per serving: calories 210, fat 4.7, fiber 2, carbs 11, protein 17

Flounder with Mushrooms

Prep time: 10 minutes I **Cooking time:** 20 minutes I **Servings:** 4

Ingredients:
- 4 flounder fillets, boneless
- 2 tablespoons olive oil
- 1 cup mushrooms, sliced
- 3 green onions, chopped
- 1 tablespoon lime juice
- ¼ teaspoon nutmeg, ground
- ¼ cup almonds, toasted and chopped
- A pinch of salt and black pepper

Directions:
1. Heat up a pan with the oil over medium-high heat, add the green onions and sauté for 5 minutes.
2. Add the mushrooms and cook for 5 minutes more.
3. Add the fish and the other ingredients, cook it for 5 minutes on each side, divide between plates and serve.

Nutrition info per serving: calories 250, fat 10, fiber 3.3, carbs 7, protein 20

Spicy Shrimp with Rice

Prep time: 10 minutes I **Cooking time:** 25 minutes I **Servings:** 4

Ingredients:
- 1 pound shrimp, peeled and deveined
- 1 cup black rice
- 2 cups chicken stock
- 4 scallions, chopped
- 1 teaspoon chili powder
- 1 teaspoon sweet paprika
- 2 tablespoons avocado oil
- A pinch of salt and black pepper

Directions:
1. Heat up a pan with the oil over medium-high heat, add the scallions and sauté for 5 minutes.
2. Add the rice and the other ingredients except the shrimp, and cook the mix for 15 minutes.
3. Add the shrimp, cook everything for another 5 minutes, divide into bowls and serve.

Nutrition info per serving: calories 240, fat 7, fiber 6, carbs 8, protein 14

Dill Sea Bass

Prep time: 5 minutes I **Cooking time:** 12 minutes I **Servings:** 4

Ingredients:
- 4 sea bass fillets, boneless
- 2 tablespoons olive oil
- 3 spring onions, chopped
- 2 tablespoons lemon juice
- Salt and black pepper to the taste
- 2 tablespoons dill, chopped

Directions:
1. Heat up a pan with the oil over medium heat, add the onions and sauté for 2 minutes.
2. Add the fish and the other ingredients, cook everything for 5 minutes on each side, divide the mix between plates and serve.

Nutrition info per serving: calories 214, fat 12, fiber 4, carbs 7, protein 17

Trout with Coconut Tomato Sauce

Prep time: 4 minutes I **Cooking time:** 15 minutes I **Servings:** 4

Ingredients:
- 4 trout fillets, boneless
- 2 spring onions, chopped
- 2 tablespoons olive oil
- 1 cup tomatoes, peeled and crushed
- ¼ cup coconut cream
- 1 tablespoon chives, chopped
- A pinch of salt and black pepper

Directions:
1. Heat up a pan with the oil over medium heat, add the spring onions, tomatoes and the cream and cook for 5 minutes.
2. Add the fish and the rest of the ingredients, toss, cook everything for 10 minutes more, divide between plates and serve.

Nutrition info per serving: calories 200, fat 5, fiber 6, carbs 12, protein 12

Salmon and Cilantro Roasted Peppers

Prep time: 5 minutes I **Cooking time:** 25 minutes I **Servings:** 4

Ingredients:
- 1 cup roasted red peppers, cut into strips
- 4 salmon fillets, boneless
- ¼ cup chicken stock
- 2 tablespoons olive oil
- 1 yellow onion, chopped
- 1 tablespoon cilantro, chopped
- A pinch of sea salt and black pepper

Directions:
1. Heat up a pan with the oil over medium-high heat, add the onion and sauté for 5 minutes.
2. Add the fish and cook for 5 minutes on each side.
3. Add the rest of the ingredients, introduce the pan in the oven and cook at 390 degrees F for 10 minutes.
4. Divide the mix between plates and serve.

Nutrition info per serving: calories 265, fat 7, fiber 5, carbs 15, protein 16

Lemon and Garlic Shrimp and Beets

Prep time: 10 minutes I **Cooking time:** 10 minutes I **Servings:** 4

Ingredients:
- 1 pound shrimp, peeled and deveined
- 2 tablespoons avocado oil
- 2 spring onions, chopped
- 2 garlic cloves, minced
- 1 beet, peeled and cubed
- 1 tablespoon lemon juice
- A pinch of sea salt and black pepper
- 1 teaspoon coconut aminos

Directions:
1. Heat up a pan with the oil over medium-high heat, add the spring onions and the garlic and sauté for 2 minutes.
2. Add the shrimp and the other ingredients, toss, cook the mix for 8 minutes, divide into bowls and serve.

Nutrition info per serving: calories 281, fat 6, fiber 7, carbs 11, protein 8

Parsley and Lime Shrimp

Prep time: 5 minutes I **Cooking time:** 10 minutes I **Servings:** 4

Ingredients:
- 1 pound shrimp, peeled and deveined
- 2 garlic cloves, minced
- 1 cup corn
- ½ cup veggie stock
- 1 bunch parsley, chopped
- Juice of 1 lime
- 2 tablespoons olive oil
- A pinch of sea salt and black pepper

Directions:
1. Heat up a pan with the oil over medium-high heat, add the garlic and the corn and sauté for 2 minutes.
2. Add the shrimp and the other ingredients, toss, cook everything for 8 minutes more, divide between plates and serve.

Nutrition info per serving: calories 345, fat 11.2, fiber 4.5, carbs 15, protein 5.6

Cumin Shrimp and Almonds

Prep time: 10 minutes I **Cooking time:** 10 minutes I **Servings:** 4

Ingredients:
- 1 pound shrimp, peeled and deveined
- 2 tablespoons chili paste
- A pinch of sea salt and black pepper
- 1 tablespoon olive oil
- 1 cup pineapple, peeled and cubed
- ½ teaspoon ginger, grated
- 2 teaspoons almonds, chopped
- 2 tablespoons cilantro, chopped

Directions:
1. Heat up a pan with the oil over medium-high heat, add the ginger and the chili paste, stir and cook for 2 minutes.
2. Add the shrimp and the other ingredients, toss, cook the mix for 8 minutes more, divide into bowls and serve.

Nutrition info per serving: calories 261, fat 4, fiber 7, carbs 15, protein 8

Tilapia and Red Beans

Prep time: 5 minutes I **Cooking time:** 20 minutes I **Servings:** 4

Ingredients:
- 1 tablespoon olive oil
- 2 tablespoons green curry paste
- 4 tilapia fillets, boneless
- Juice of ½ lime
- 1 cup red kidney beans, cooked
- 1 tablespoon parsley, chopped

Directions:
1. Heat up a pan with the oil over medium heat, add the fish and cook for 5 minutes on each side.
2. Add the rest of the ingredients, toss gently, cook over medium heat for 10 minutes more, divide between plates and serve.

Nutrition info per serving: calories 271, fat 4, fiber 6, carbs 14, protein 7

Shrimp with Corn and Olives

Prep time: 5 minutes I **Cooking time:** 10 minutes I **Servings:** 4

Ingredients:
- 2 tablespoons olive oil
- 1 pound shrimp, peeled and deveined
- 1 teaspoon rosemary, dried
- 1 cup corn
- 1 cup black olives, pitted and halved
- 1 teaspoon smoked paprika
- A pinch of sea salt and black pepper

Directions:
1. Heat up a pan with the oil over medium-high heat, add the shrimp, rosemary and the other ingredients, toss, cook for 10 minutes, divide into bowls and serve.

Nutrition info per serving: calories 271, fat 4, fiber 6, carbs 14, protein 15

Citrus Scallops

Prep time: 5 minutes I **Cooking time:** 10 minutes I **Servings:** 4

Ingredients:
- 1 pound sea scallops
- 4 scallions, chopped
- 2 tablespoons olive oil
- 1 tablespoon orange juice
- 1 tablespoon cilantro, chopped
- A pinch of salt and black pepper

Directions:
1. Heat up a pan with the oil over medium-high heat, add the scallops, the scallions and the other ingredients, toss, cook for 10 minutes, divide into bowls and serve.

Nutrition info per serving: calories 300, fat 4, fiber 4, carbs 14, protein 17

Shrimp with Leeks and Carrots

Prep time: 5 minutes I **Cooking time:** 10 minutes I **Servings:** 4

Ingredients:
- 1 pound shrimp, peeled and deveined
- 1 cup leeks, sliced
- 2 tablespoons olive oil
- ¼ cup vegetable stock
- 2 tablespoons rosemary, chopped
- 2 cups baby carrots, peeled
- 1 tablespoon lime juice
- A pinch of sea salt and black pepper

Directions:
1. Heat up a pan with the oil over medium-high heat, add the carrots, rosemary and the other ingredients except the shrimp, toss and cook for 5 minutes.
2. Add the shrimp, cook the mix for 5 minutes more, divide into bowls and serve.

Nutrition info per serving: calories 271, fat 6, fiber 7, carbs 14, protein 18

Cod and Barley

Prep time: 10 minutes I **Cooking time:** 25 minutes I **Servings:** 4

Ingredients:
- 3 scallions, chopped
- 2 cups chicken stock
- 1 pound cod fillets, boneless and cubed
- 1 cup barley
- 2 tablespoons olive oil
- 2 celery stalks, chopped
- A pinch of salt and black pepper
- 1 tablespoon coriander, chopped

Directions:
1. Heat up a pan with the oil over medium-high heat, add the scallions and the celery and sauté for 5 minutes.
2. Add the fish and cook for 5 minutes more.
3. Add the rest of the ingredients, toss, cook over medium heat for 15 minutes more, divide everything between plates and serve.

Nutrition info per serving: calories 261, fat 4, fiber 6, carbs 14, protein 7

Shrimp and Balsamic Sweet Peppers

Prep time: 5 minutes I **Cooking time:** 12 minutes I **Servings:** 4

Ingredients:
- 1 pound shrimp, peeled and deveined
- 2 tablespoons avocado oil
- 2 spring onions, chopped
- 2 sweet peppers, cut into strips
- 1 tablespoon balsamic vinegar
- 1 tablespoon chives, minced
- A pinch of sea salt and black pepper

Directions:
1. Heat up a pan with the oil over medium-high heat, add the spring onions, peppers and chives, stir and cook for 4 minutes.
2. Add the shrimp and the rest of the ingredients, toss, cook over medium heat for 8 minutes more, divide into bowls and serve.

Nutrition info per serving: calories 191, fat 3.3, fiber 8,5 carbs 11.3, protein 29.3

Cumin Snapper Mix

Prep time: 5 minutes I **Cooking time:** 20 minutes I **Servings:** 4

Ingredients:
- 2 tablespoons olive oil
- 2 garlic cloves, minced
- 4 snapper fillets, boneless, skinless and cubed
- 1 tomato, cubed
- 1 zucchini, cubed
- 1 tablespoon coriander, chopped
- ½ teaspoon cumin, ground
- ½ teaspoon rosemary, dried
- A pinch of salt and black pepper

Directions:
1. Heat up a pan with the oil over medium-high heat, add the garlic, tomato and zucchini and cook for 5 minutes.
2. Add the fish and the other ingredients, toss, cook the mix for 15 minutes more, divide it into bowls and serve.

Nutrition info per serving: calories 251, fat 4, fiber 6, carbs 14, protein 7

Masala Scallops

Prep time: 10 minutes I **Cooking time:** 20 minutes I **Servings:** 4

Ingredients:
- 2 tablespoons olive oil
- 2 jalapenos, chopped
- 1 pound sea scallops
- A pinch of salt and black pepper
- ¼ teaspoon cinnamon powder
- 1 teaspoon garam masala
- 1 teaspoon coriander, ground
- 1 teaspoon cumin, ground
- 2 tablespoons cilantro, chopped

Directions:
1. Heat up a pan with the oil over medium heat, add the jalapenos, cinnamon and the other ingredients except the scallops and cook for 10 minutes.
2. Add the rest of the ingredients, toss, cook for 10 minutes more, divide into bowls and serve.

Nutrition info per serving: calories 251, fat 4, fiber 4, carbs 11, protein 17

Cinnamon Tuna

Prep time: 5 minutes I **Cooking time:** 20 minutes I **Servings:** 4

Ingredients:
- 1 yellow onion, chopped
- 1 tablespoon olive oil
- 1 pound tuna fillets, boneless, skinless and cubed
- 1 tablespoon cinnamon powder
- 1 red pepper, chopped
- 1 teaspoon sweet paprika
- 1 tablespoon coriander, chopped

Directions:
1. Heat up a pan with the oil over medium heat, add the onions and the pepper and cook for 5 minutes.
2. Add the fish and the other ingredients, cook everything for 15 minutes, divide between plates and serve.

Nutrition info per serving: calories 215, fat 4, fiber 7, carbs 14, protein 7

Tuna and Kale

Prep time: 5 minutes I **Cooking time:** 20 minutes I **Servings:** 4

Ingredients:
- 1 pound tuna fillets, boneless, skinless and cubed
- A pinch of salt and black pepper
- 2 tablespoons olive oil
- 1 cup kale, torn
- ½ cup cherry tomatoes, cubed
- 1 yellow onion, chopped

Directions:
1. Heat up a pan with the oil over medium heat, add the onion and sauté for 5 minutes.
2. Add the tuna and the other ingredients, toss, cook everything for 15 minutes more, divide between plates and serve.

Nutrition info per serving: calories 251, fat 4, fiber 7, carbs 14, protein 7

Lemongrass Mackerel

Prep time: 10 minutes I **Cooking time:** 25 minutes I **Servings:** 4

Ingredients:
- 4 mackerel fillets, skinless and boneless
- 2 tablespoons olive oil
- 1 tablespoon ginger, grated
- 2 lemongrass sticks, chopped
- 2 red chilies, chopped
- Juice of 1 lime
- A handful parsley, chopped

Directions:
1. In a roasting pan, combine the mackerel with the oil, ginger and the other ingredients, toss and bake at 390 degrees F for 25 minutes.
2. Divide everything between plates and serve.

Nutrition info per serving: calories 251, fat 3, fiber 4, carbs 14, protein 8

Scallops with Almonds

Prep time: 5 minutes I **Cooking time:** 10 minutes I **Servings:** 4

Ingredients:
- 1 pound scallops
- 2 tablespoons olive oil
- 4 scallions, chopped
- A pinch of salt and black pepper
- ½ cup mushrooms, sliced
- 2 tablespoon almonds, chopped
- 1 cup coconut cream

Directions:
1. Heat up a pan with the oil over medium heat, add the scallions and the mushrooms and sauté for 2 minutes.
2. Add the scallops and the other ingredients, toss, cook over medium heat for 8 minutes more, divide into bowls and serve.

Nutrition info per serving: calories 322, fat 23.7, fiber 2.2, carbs 8.1, protein 21.6

Scallops and Leeks

Prep time: 5 minutes I **Cooking time:** 22 minutes I **Servings:** 4

Ingredients:
- 1 pound scallops
- ½ teaspoon rosemary, dried
- ½ teaspoon oregano, dried
- 2 tablespoons avocado oil
- 1 yellow onion, chopped
- 2 leeks, sliced
- ½ cup chicken stock
- 1 tablespoon cilantro, chopped
- A pinch of salt and black pepper

Directions:
1. Heat up a pan with the oil over medium heat, add the onion and sauté for 2 minutes.
2. Add the leeks and the stock, toss and cook for 10 minutes more.
3. Add the scallops and the remaining ingredients, toss, cook for another 10 minutes, divide everything into bowls and serve.

Nutrition info per serving: calories 211, fat 2, fiber 4.1, carbs 26.9, protein 20.7

Salmon and BroccoliSalad

Prep time: 5 minutes I **Cooking time:** 0 minutes I **Servings:** 4

Ingredients:
- 1 cup smoked salmon, boneless and flaked
- 1 cup broccoli florets, cooked
- ½ cup baby arugula
- 1 tablespoon lemon juice
- 2 spring onions, chopped
- 1 tablespoon olive oil
- A pinch of sea salt and black pepper

Directions:
1. In a salad bowl, combine the salmon with the broccoli and the other ingredients, toss and serve.

Nutrition info per serving: calories 210, fat 6, fiber 5, carbs 10, protein 12

Shrimp and Dates Salad

Prep time: 10 minutes I **Cooking time:** 0 minutes I **Servings:** 4

Ingredients:
- 1 pound shrimp, cooked, peeled and deveined
- 2 cups baby spinach
- 2 tablespoons walnuts, chopped
- 1 cup cherry tomatoes, halved
- 1 tablespoon lemon juice
- ½ cup dates, chopped
- 2 tablespoons avocado oil

Directions:
1. In a salad bowl, mix the shrimp with the spinach, walnuts and the other ingredients, toss and serve.

Nutrition info per serving: calories 243, fat 5.4, fiber 3.3, carbs 21.6, protein 28.3

Salmon and Watercress Bowls

Prep time: 10 minutes I **Cooking time:** 0 minutes I **Servings:** 4

Ingredients:
- 1 pound smoked salmon, boneless, skinless and flaked
- 2 spring onions, chopped
- 2 tablespoons avocado oil
- ½ cup baby arugula
- 1 cup watercress
- 1 tablespoon lemon juice
- 1 cucumber, sliced
- 1 avocado, peeled, pitted and roughly cubed
- A pinch of sea salt and black pepper

Directions:
1. In a salad bowl, mix the salmon with the spring onions, watercress and the other ingredients, toss and serve.

Nutrition info per serving: calories 261, fat 15.8, fiber 4.4, carbs 8.2, protein 22.7

Trout and Butter Sauce

Prep time: 10 minutes I **Cooking time:** 10 minutes I **Servings:** 4

Ingredients:

- 4 trout fillets
- Salt and ground black pepper, to taste
- 3 teaspoons lemon zest, grated
- 3 tablespoons fresh chives, chopped
- 6 tablespoons butter
- 2 tablespoons olive oil
- 2 teaspoons lemon juice

Directions:
1. Season trout with salt, pepper, drizzle olive oil, and massage into fish.
2. Heat a kitchen grill over medium–high heat, add fish fillets, cook for 4 minutes, flip, and cook for 4 minutes.
3. Heat a pan with the butter over medium heat, add salt, pepper, chives, lemon juice, lemon zest, and stir well.
4. Divide fish fillets on plates, drizzle the butter sauce over them, and serve.

Nutrition info per serving: Calories – 333, Fat – 29.6, Fiber – 0.2, Carbs – 0.5, Protein – 16.8

Kimchi Salmon

Prep time: 10 minutes I **Cooking time:** 12 minutes I **Servings:** 4

Ingredients:

- 2 tablespoons butter, softened
- 1¼ pound salmon fillet
- 2 ounces kimchi, diced
- Salt and ground black pepper, to taste

Directions:
1. In a food processor, mix butter with kimchi and blend well.
2. Rub salmon with salt, pepper, and kimchi mixture, and place into a baking dish.
3. Place in an oven at 425ºF and bake for 15 minutes. Divide on plates and serve.

Nutrition info per serving: Calories – 467, Fat – 25, Fiber – 0, Carbs – 0.5, Protein – 60.6

Salmon Meatballs and Sauce

Prep time: 10 minutes I **Cooking time:** 30 minutes I **Servings:** 4

Ingredients:

- 2 tablespoons butter
- 2 garlic cloves, peeled and minced
- ⅓ cup onion, peeled and chopped
- 1 pound wild salmon, boneless and minced
- ¼ cup fresh chives, chopped
- 1 egg
- 2 tablespoons Dijon mustard
- 1 tablespoon coconut flour
- Salt and ground black pepper, to taste

For the sauce:

- 4 garlic cloves, peeled and minced
- 2 tablespoons butter
- 2 tablespoons Dijon mustard
- Juice, and zest of 1 lemon
- 2 cups coconut cream
- 2 tablespoons fresh chives, chopped

Directions:

1. Heat a pan with 2 tablespoons butter over medium heat, add onion and 2 garlic cloves, stir, cook for 3 minutes, and transfer to a bowl.
2. In another bowl, mix the onion and garlic with salmon, chives, coconut flour, salt, pepper, 2 tablespoons mustard, egg, and stir well.
3. Shape meatballs from salmon mixture, place on a baking sheet, place in an oven at 350ºF, and bake for 25 minutes.
4. Heat a pan with 2 tablespoons butter over medium heat, add 4 garlic cloves, stir, and cook for 1 minute.
5. Add coconut cream, 2 tablespoons Dijon mustard, lemon juice, lemon zest, chives, stir, and cook for 3 minutes.
6. Take salmon meatballs out of the oven, drop them into the Dijon sauce, toss, cook for 1 minute, and take off the heat. Divide into bowls and serve.

Nutrition info per serving: Calories – 575, Fat – 47.1, Fiber – 3.4, Carbs – 9, Protein – 31.9

Baked Lemon Haddock

Prep time: 10 minutes I **Cooking time:** 30 minutes I **Servings:** 4

Ingredients:

- 1 pound haddock
- 3 teaspoons water
- 2 tablespoons lemon juice
- Salt and ground black pepper, to taste
- 2 tablespoons mayonnaise
- 1 teaspoon dill weed
- Vegetable oil cooking spray
- A pinch of Old Bay Seasoning

Directions:
1. Spray a baking dish with some cooking oil.
2. Add lemon juice, water, fish, and toss to coat. Add salt, pepper, Old Bay Seasoning, dill, and toss again. Add mayonnaise and spread well.
3. Place in an oven at 350ºF, and bake for 30 minutes. Divide on plates and serve.

Nutrition info per serving: Calories – 121, Fat – 3.5, Fiber – 0, Carbs – 1.9, Protein – 20.1

Tilapia and Mayo Mix

Prep time: 10 minutes I **Cooking time:** 10 minutes I **Servings:** 4

Ingredients:

- 4 tilapia fillets, boneless
- Salt and ground black pepper, to taste
- ½ cup Parmesan cheese, grated
- 4 tablespoons mayonnaise
- ¼ teaspoon dried basil
- ¼ teaspoon garlic powder
- 2 tablespoons lemon juice
- ¼ cup butter
- Vegetable oil cooking spray
- A pinch of onion powder

Directions:

1. Spray a baking sheet with cooking spray, and arrange the tilapia on the tray.
2. Season with salt, pepper, place under a preheated broiler, and cook for 3 minutes.
3. Turn the fish and broil for 3 minutes.
4. In a bowl, mix Parmesan cheese with mayonnaise, basil, garlic, lemon juice, onion powder, butter, and stir well.
5. Add fish to mixture, toss to coat well, place on baking sheet again, and broil for 3 minutes. Transfer to plates and serve.

Nutrition info per serving: calories 300, fat 20.5, fiber 0.1, carbs 4.3, protein 25.9

Trout and Pecan Sauce

Prep time: 10 minutes I **Cooking time:** 10 minutes I **Servings:** 1

Ingredients:

- 1 trout fillet
- Salt and ground black pepper, to taste
- 1 tablespoon olive oil
- 1 tablespoon butter
- Zest, and juice from 1 lemon
- ½ cup fresh parsley, chopped
- ½ cup pecans, chopped

Directions:
1. Heat a pan with the oil over medium–high heat, add fish fillet, season with salt, pepper, cook for 4 minutes on each side, transfer to a plate and keep warm.
2. Heat the same pan with butter over medium heat, add pecans, stir, and toast for 1 minutes.
3. Add lemon juice, lemon zest, some salt, pepper, and chopped parsley, stir, cook for 1 minute, and pour over the fish fillets, and serve.

Nutrition info per serving: calories 838, fat 81, fiber 8.5, carbs 11.9, protein 25

Salmon with Butter Caper Sauce

Prep time: 10 minutes I **Cooking time:** 20 minutes I **Servings:** 3

Ingredients:

- 3 salmon fillets
- Salt and ground black pepper, to taste
- 1 tablespoon olive oil
- 1 tablespoon Italian seasoning
- 2 tablespoons capers
- 3 tablespoons lemon juice
- 4 garlic cloves, peeled and minced
- 2 tablespoons butter

Directions:
1. Heat a pan with olive oil over medium heat, add fish fillets skin side up, season with salt, pepper, and Italian seasoning, cook for 2 minutes, flip, and cook for 2 minutes, take off heat, cover pan, and set aside for 15 minutes.
2. Transfer fish to a plate, and leave them aside.
3. Heat the same pan over medium heat, add capers, lemon juice, and garlic, stir, and cook for 2 minutes.
4. Take pan off the heat, add the butter, and stir well.
5. Return fish to pan, and toss to coat with the sauce. Divide on plates and serve.

Nutrition info per serving: Calories – 369, Fat – 24.9, Fiber – 0.3, Carbs – 2.4, Protein – 35.

1

Grilled Oysters

Prep time: 10 minutes I **Cooking time:** 10 minutes I **Servings:** 3

Ingredients:

- 6 oysters, shucked
- 3 garlic cloves, peeled and minced
- 1 lemon, cut in wedges
- 1 tablespoon parsley
- A pinch of sweet paprika
- 2 tablespoons melted butter

Directions:
1. Top each oyster with melted butter, parsley, paprika, and butter.
2. Place on preheated grill pan over medium–high heat, and cook for 8 minutes.
3. Serve them with lemon wedges on the side.

Nutrition info per serving: Calories – 272, Fat – 15.7, Fiber – 0.1, Carbs – 13, Protein – 20.3

Baked Butter Halibut

Prep time: 10 minutes I **Cooking time:** 10 minutes I **Servings:** 4

Ingredients:

- ½ cup Parmesan cheese, grated
- ¼ cup butter
- 2 tablespoons green onions, chopped
- 6 garlic cloves, peeled and minced
- A dash of Tabasco sauce
- 4 halibut fillets, boneless
- Salt and ground black pepper, to taste
- Juice of ½ lemon

Directions:

1. Season halibut with salt, pepper, and some of the lemon juice, place in a baking dish, and cook in the oven at 450ºF for 6 minutes.
2. Heat a pan with butter over medium heat, add Parmesan cheese, mayonnaise, green onions, Tabasco sauce, garlic, remaining lemon juice, and stir well.
3. Take fish out of the oven, drizzle cheese sauce all over, turn the oven to broil, and broil the fish for 3 minutes. Divide on plates and serve.

Nutrition info per serving: Calories – 530, Fat – 26.2, Fiber – 0.2, Carbs – 5.7, Protein – 65.6

Herbed Tuna Cakes

Prep time: 10 minutes I **Cooking time:** 10 minutes I **Servings:** 12

Ingredients:

- 15 ounces smoked tuna, flaked
- 3 eggs
- ½ teaspoon dried dill
- 1 teaspoon dried parsley
- ½ cup onion chopped
- 1 teaspoon garlic powder
- Salt and ground black pepper, to taste
- Oil, for frying

Directions:

1. In a bowl, mix tuna with salt, pepper, dill, parsley, onion, garlic powder, eggs, and stir well.
2. Shape tuna cakes and place on a plate.
3. Heat a pan with oil over medium–high heat, add tuna cakes, cook for 5 minutes on each side. Divide on plates and serve.

Nutrition info per serving: Calories – 84, Fat – 4, Fiber – 0.1, Carbs – 0.6, Protein – 10.8

CPSIA information can be obtained
at www.ICGtesting.com
Printed in the USA
LVHW051107241220
675071LV00004B/651